SANTA MONICA
PUBLIC
LIBRARY

www.smpl.org

4-WEEK LOAN

TELEPHONE RENEWALS:
Main Library. 451-1866
Ocean Park Branch. 392-3804
Fairview Branch 450-0443
Montana Branch 829-7081

DATE DUE

APR 2 5 2005	

Soldiers and Their Families
of the California Mission Frontier

Jack S. Williams
Thomas L. Davis

The Rosen Publishing Group's
PowerKids Press™
New York

To the descendants of California's first settlers

Published in 2003 by The Rosen Publishing Group, Inc.
29 East 21st Street, New York, NY 10010

First Edition

Editor: Joanne Randolph
Book Design: Corinne Jacob

Photo Credits: Cover, pp. 19, 28, 34, 44, drawings by Father Ignacio Tirsch, courtesy of the National Library of the Czech Republic; pp. 4, 6 © Archivo Iconografico, S.A./CORBIS; pp. 8–9, 15 illustrated by Jack Williams; p. 10 courtesy of the Serra Cause, Old Mission Santa Barbara; pp. 11, 12, 13, 21, 32, 47, 49, 50, 51, 56 courtesy of Jack Williams; p. 16 Library of Congress, Geography and Map Division; pp. 22, 40 © George Ancona; pp. 24, 57 original art reference by Jack Williams, recreation by Corinne Jacob; p. 27 courtesy of the Bancroft Library, University of California; p. 31 courtesy of the California History Room, California State Library, Sacramento, California; p. 36 Richard Beechy, "Mission of San Carlos, Monterey," 1827, watercolor, Autry Museum of Western Heritage, Los Angeles; p. 41 courtesy of La Purisima Mission, State Historic Park, California, photo © Cristina Taccone; p. 55 "El Hacendero y su mayordomo" by Carl Nebel, courtesy of the General Libraries, the University of Texas at Austin.

Williams, Jack S.
Soldiers and their families of the California mission frontier / Jack S. Williams and Thomas L. Davis.— 1st ed.
   p. cm. — (People of the California missions)
Includes bibliographical references and index.
ISBN 0-8239-6285-7 (lib. bdg.)
1. California—History—To 1846—Juvenile literature. 2. Missions, Spanish—California—History—Juvenile literature. 3. Soldiers—California—History—Juvenile literature. 4. Soldiers—California—Family relationships—History—Juvenile literature. 5. Spaniards—California—History—Juvenile literature. 6. Spain—Colonies—America—Administration—Juvenile literature. 7. California—Social life and customs—Juvenile literature. 8. Frontier and pioneer life—California—Juvenile literature. [1. California—History—To 1846. 2. Missions—California—History. 3. Soldiers—History—19th century. 4. Soldiers—Family relationships—History. 5. Spaniards—California—History. 6. Spain—Colonies—America. 7. California—Social life and customs. 8. Frontier and pioneer life—California.] I. Davis, Thomas L. (Thomas Leslie), 1960– II. Title.
F864 .W73 2003
979.4'04—dc21

2001004326

Manufactured in the United States of America

Contents

1. The California Mission Frontier 5

2. Digging Up the Past 11

3. The Spanish Army in California .14

4. A Soldier's Life in the Ranks 21

5. A Soldier's Life Off Duty 30

6. A Soldier's Life at the Missions 37

7. The Women of the Military Families 39

8. Growing Up in a Military Family 43

9. Religion and the Military Families 49

10. Leaving the Army 54

   Glossary 58

   Additional Resources 61

   Index 62

The California Mission Frontier

Before Europeans reached the shores of America, there was no place known as California, although the lands that would one day be included in the modern state did exist. Just as today, this was a place of towering mountains, burning deserts, dense forests, and vast grasslands. Not only did the land exist before Europeans arrived, but people already lived there, too. Hidden along the shorelines of the Pacific Ocean were many different groups of Native Americans. In the south were the Kumeyaay, the Cahuilla, and the Tongva. Along the central coast were the Chumash and the Salinans. In the north were the Esselen, the Ohlone, the Wintun, the Wappo, and the Coast Miwok. In the interior, there were many other groups, including the Quechan, the Serrano, the Chemeuvi, the Yokuts, and the Mojaves. Each group followed different customs, spoke a different language, and worshiped different gods.

During the first century of European expansion into the Americas, the outside world started to learn about the place that would later become known as California. Hernán Cortés, the conqueror of ancient Mexico, gave the region its name based on the story of Califia, a legendary Amazon queen. Before 1550, explorers had touched on the western shores of what they called Alta California, or Upper California. By 1600, European ships often sailed down the coastline as they made their way from the Philippines to

◄ *An artist by the name of M. Se Colane painted this sixteenth-century portrait of Hernán Cortés (1485-1547), the Spanish soldier who conquered Mexico for Spain. Cortés's coat of arms is in the upper left corner of the painting.*

 5

This portrait of Carlos III was painted by Andres de la Calleja during the eighteenth century. Carlos III was the king of Spain from 1759 to 1788. He wanted California to be under Spanish rule.

Mexico. The sailors on board these vessels sometimes stopped to explore, but they did not come to stay. The Indian people sometimes traded with the strangers, but for the most part things went on as they had before the Europeans arrived.

All of this began to change in the middle of the eighteenth century. In Europe, rival kings were laying claim to the "unoccupied" lands of America. Carlos III, king of Spain, argued that he owned all of California. However, the Indians that lived there did not accept him, or anyone else, as their master. There were men living in other nations who also dreamed of making California their colony. English and Russian politicians wanted the region for their own empires. José de Gálvez, a Spanish official, had been placed in charge of the defense of the Spanish colony of

Mexico by Carlos III. To Gálvez it seemed Spain would have to act soon or give up her claims forever.

There was a problem, however. Spain did not have the resources to launch a new colony. The nation lacked people, money, and especially soldiers. How could Gálvez hope to occupy California and protect it from the Russians and the English? It was a question that had no easy answer.

Gálvez finally came up with a daring plan. The Spaniards would teach the Indians the European way of life. As in other parts of northern New Spain, or modern-day northern Mexico and the United States's Southwest, the king would colonize the region using missions. A handful of Roman Catholic Franciscan priests, headed by Father Junípero Serra, would establish these communities. There the missionaries would transform the Indian people into loyal Spanish settlers. In the eyes of the government and the Franciscans, only a person who believed in the Roman Catholic religion was a "civilized person." Therefore, the people in the province had to become Christians. Though today we embrace people's differences, colonial governments during the eighteenth century often oppressed their subjects. The hope was that the Indians would become colonists and would protect California for the king of Spain. Eventually they would become prosperous and would send money to the Crown in the form of taxes.

Gálvez realized that Spanish California was going to be a dangerous place. To protect the missions, he decided that the king needed to build a chain of presidios. Each presidio was a military colony protected by fortifications.

Soldiers and their families would live at these outposts. There were not enough troops to send a big army to the region, so none of the presidios would have many soldiers. The lack of funds meant that the troops and their families would have to be largely self-sufficient, raising most of their own food and building their homes using the things that they could find in California.

Perhaps the most difficult challenge faced by Gálvez was that no trails connected California with the southern Spanish colonies, such as Mexico.

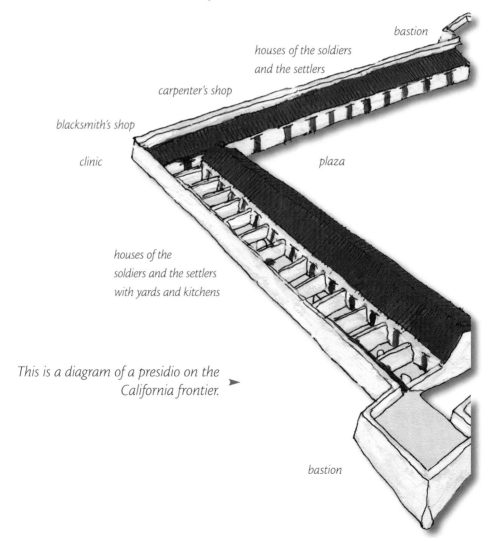

bastion

houses of the soldiers
and the settlers

carpenter's shop

blacksmith's shop

clinic

plaza

houses of the
soldiers and the settlers
with yards and kitchens

This is a diagram of a presidio on the California frontier. ➤

bastion

The first colonists would have to travel across a large area of unexplored desert to reach their new homes. This place would have seemed unfamiliar and strange to them. The expedition launched in 1769, with fewer than 300 people. More than half of these people died during the next two years. Even so, the Spaniards did not give up. By 1823, they had established a series of 21 missions, four presidios, and three towns, or pueblos.

Not everything was as secure as Spain wanted, however. While Father Serra built his missions, on the other side of the continent men like George

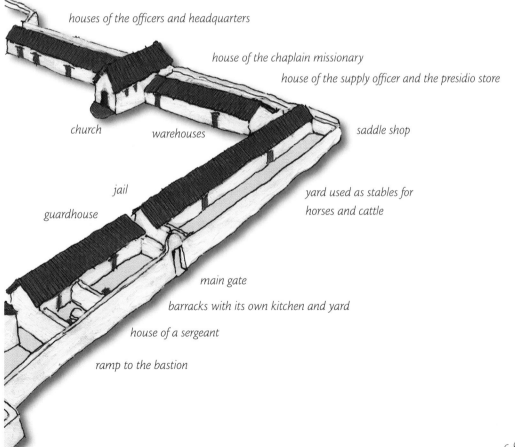

houses of the officers and headquarters

house of the chaplain missionary

house of the supply officer and the presidio store

church   warehouses   saddle shop

jail

guardhouse   yard used as stables for horses and cattle

main gate

barracks with its own kitchen and yard

house of a sergeant

ramp to the bastion

Father Junípero Serra (1713–1784) was a Spanish missionary called the Apostle of California. He entered the Franciscan order in 1730, and went to lower California in 1767. Serra founded numerous missions and also worked to protect the rights of Indians. This illustration of Father Serra was created in the 1800s.

Washington and Thomas Jefferson were winning a war of independence against Britain. Out of this struggle, 13 colonies would become the United States. Between 1810 and 1821, Mexico followed a similar path, and in 1821, Mexico became an independent nation. Soon government support for the missions came to an end. The lack of government funding for the army also caused the abandonment of the presidios. By 1835, the Spanish system of colonization had ended. The glory days of the presidios and the missions passed into memory. When California was added to the United States in 1846, the missions and the presidios had already fallen into ruins.

Digging Up the Past

This is a button that was worn by a Spanish soldier or settler. The buttons were originally created for the use of Haitian troops, but were later imported to California by British manufacturers.

The last person to have lived in one of California's Spanish presidios has been dead for more than 100 years. All that is left of those distant times are some crumbling documents, broken objects like pottery, and melted walls. We have no time machines that allow us to visit the past. To figure out the mystery of what happened so long ago, we have to turn to the methods of science. We have to gather evidence and work as detectives to figure out what happened in history.

Many different kinds of researchers work at gathering and studying the evidence. Historians study the photographs, the written records, and the stories left behind by earlier generations. Anthropologists study the customs of living people to learn more about how things were done in the past. Other researchers create copies of old tools and weapons. They attempt to make these work to see what kind of technology was available to help people live, work, and play in the past. They can also discover what the tool's purpose might have been. Archaeologists study the traces of earlier human activities.

Specialists known as historical archaeologists excavate Spanish colonial sites, such as missions and presidios. The people that lived at these outposts did not

always write down information about what they were doing. Nevertheless, they left behind other clues. The archaeologists discover details about many of these activities by studying artifacts. An artifact is any item that shows evidence of people's presence. An archaeologist can often tell you a lot about what people ate and what they did to make a living by analyzing artifacts, such as the tools and the animal bones that they discover. Each archaeological site represents a complex puzzle. In California, the discovery of different kinds

Archaeologists work slowly using small tools to uncover artifacts. Brushes are used to uncover delicate items.

of pottery helps the researchers to identify particular time periods. Historical archaeologists have to work very hard to figure out what it was like to live long ago.

◄ *If an archaeologist discovers a lot of decorated pottery pieces made in Mexico at a California presidio, it suggests that the things found around it may date to before 1800.*

The Spanish Army in California

If we compare the size of the army stationed in California with the size of the army dedicated to protecting the other parts of the Spanish Empire, then it becomes clear why it is so hard to find traces of the soldiers. There were never more than 500 soldiers assigned to protect California at any given time. This tiny force lived in four presidios. San Diego was founded in 1769. Santa Bárbara was founded in 1782. Monterey was founded in 1770, and San Francisco was founded in 1776.

Why did the king of Spain assign soldiers to protect California? Although the Crown was committed to a program of peaceful mission expansion, there were a number of things that made the government send men to guard the province. Many of the officials were afraid that either the Russians or the English would invade California. Even if the mission Indians had defended the region, the king's representatives were scared that the native peoples and the Franciscans lacked the training and the weapons to win. The government officials were also afraid that some of the Indians might attack the missionaries. Hostile Indians had driven the priests away in other frontier regions. The Crown also wanted to make sure that a governor named by the king, and not the Franciscans, would run the province. The king needed soldiers in California to protect his interests.

The army stationed in California was split between four presidios, at San Francisco, Santa Bárbara, Monterey, and San Diego. Their job was to protect the mission communities.

A New & Correct MAP of the

WHOLE WORLD

Shewing ye Situation of its Principal Parts. Viz the
Seas, Kingdoms, Rivers, Capes, Ports, Mountains,
Woods, Trade-Winds, Monsoons, Variation of ye Com-
pass, Climes, &c.

The Projection of this Map is Call'd Mercator's ~ the Designe is to
make it Usefull both for Land & Sea. And it is laid Down with
all possible Care, according to ye Newest & Most Exact Observations

By HERMAN MOLL Geographer 1719.

Where did the soldiers come from? The Spanish Empire stretched around the globe. It included large parts of South America, North America, Asia, Africa, and Europe. Very few of the soldiers assigned to protect the overseas colonies were born in Spain. Instead they represented the children, the grandchildren, and the great-grandchildren of earlier generations of Spanish colonists. Most of the men who served in California were descendants of other northern frontier settlers living in Sonora and Baja California. The first Spaniards who arrived in these areas had married Indians and free blacks. Some of the African peoples' ancestors had moved to Spain in the Middle Ages. Others had been captured in wars and brought to America as slaves. These people had saved enough money to purchase their freedom before moving to the frontier. Some of the Indians who lived in Sonora and Baja California moved there from other parts of Mexico. A few of the soldiers' ancestors were Asian. They came from the Philippines, another part of the world that was ruled by the king of Spain. The Asian settlers included both Filipinos and Chinese. All the people who lived on the frontier usually referred to themselves as *norteños*, or northerners.

How did a person join the army? The troops' commanders recruited the common soldiers. Normally the officer in charge of a presidio would visit the nearby towns and would set up a wooden table and a flag. A secretary and a payroll officer helped the commander to sign up recruits. The men joined for many reasons. Some wanted to go on an adventure. Others were attracted by the promise of small land grants and retirement benefits. A few of the men joined to escape trouble at home. Once they joined, they received a large cash

◄ *The Spanish Empire included lands in Europe, North America, South America, Africa, and Asia, much of which is visible in this 1719 map by Herman Moll.*

 17

bonus. The recruiters wrote down the men's names and their descriptions in a big book. After that the men signed their names, or made their marks. Then they were soldiers.

Most of the officers came from wealthy families. A person's parents usually made the decision that their son was going to join. Most wealthy people considered it a matter of pride that they fought for the king. Someone who served as a commander could go on to become an important government official. A person placed in charge of a presidio could also make a lot of money running the presidio's general store. This store was the only place that one could buy things from outside of California, and everyone shopped there. The base commanders got to keep the profits.

If a person wanted to become an officer, he or his family had to spend a lot of money. Some of the wealthy frontier families sent their young sons to become cadets. The older presidio officers trained them for future employment as commanders. The families paid for the cadets' equipment, food, and housing. Many of the officers paid a huge amount of money to the king to receive their commission, a special document making them officers. Sometimes a common soldier who showed unusual talents was given a special commission.

Most men that served in California were called *soldados de cuera*, or leather jacket soldiers. They were part of a special group of frontier cavalry armed with lances, swords, muskets, and pistols. Leather armor and shields protected these men when they went into combat. Small groups of other kinds of troops joined the leather jacket soldiers. These men used cannons,

hat

cuera, or leather jacket

carbine, or rifle

shield

stirrup

sword

A California leather jacket soldier, drawn by Ignacio Tirsch around 1765, sits on his horse.

muskets, pistols, and swords. Soldiers or their families had to buy the soldiers' weapons and equipment. Each man wore a uniform with brass buttons. Each wore a black hat, a pair of shoes, a vest, a coat, and a pair of knee-length pants.

Just as in modern armies, there were many different levels, or ranks, of soldiers in California. The governor, usually a colonel, was the highest-ranking person. Beneath him were the presidio commanders, usually captains or lieutenants. A man called an *alférez*, who carried the presidio flag into battle, assisted the commanders. Low-ranking officers called sergeants and corporals supervised the common soldiers.

Each presidio had a company, or group, of from 25 to 100 soldiers. A dozen of the men usually stayed at the presidio. The rest worked away from their bases. The soldiers had to protect the missions, ranchos, or livestock ranches, and pueblos in the surrounding areas. They also carried the mail and had many other jobs that took them into the countryside.

The soldiers had many duties that did not involve fighting. They were not just the protectors of the presidios and other California settlements. The presidios were their homes. The soldiers and their families were supposed to live and work as colonists. Most troops that served in other parts of the Spanish Empire had to live in barracks, and they were not allowed to get married. The frontier soldiers, on the other hand, brought their families with them to live in private homes at the presidios. They worked hard to raise cattle and crops on their small land grants. Hoping to expand the Spanish Empire, the king wanted the soldiers to build presidios that were as much towns as they were forts. Retired soldiers did not return to homes or to families left behind. They lived at the bases and in other nearby Spanish settlements.

The soldiers received a modest amount of pay. Part of their salary went to retirement and to healthcare. They raised their own food and made most of their own clothes, so the men and their families did not have to spend very much on necessities. Instead they used their pay to buy luxury goods at the general store. A small amount of cash was usually saved for emergencies.

A Soldier's Life in the Ranks

California soldiers faced many challenges and dangerous situations. Each day the men would rise from their beds to the sound of the morning assembly bell. They would eat breakfast and then would come together on the main plaza of the presidio. The officer in charge would read off the duty assignments, and the men would proceed to their work. At about 12:00 P.M., the presidio bell would sound again. The soldiers and the rest of the colonists would eat the main meal of the day, and then take a siesta, or afternoon rest. This break would last until about 3:00 P.M. During this time period, the soldiers could sleep, relax, or do anything else that they wanted to do. The bell would ring once more and the men would return to work for the remaining hours of the day. Afterward the soldiers had their evenings to themselves. They usually ate dinner and visited with family and friends. Most went to bed between 12:00 A.M. and 2:00 A.M. Every man was responsible for showing up the next day ready for a new assignment.

Training

As did soldiers everywhere, the men spent hour after hour in training exercises. It took years of hard work to become a

The men had to play and ➤
recognize many drum calls.

frontier soldier. Nearly all the men were already excellent horsemen and cowboys. Once they were in the army, they had to learn to march, to ride horses, and to fight as part of a team.

The soldiers were drilled heavily in the use of their weapons. The sergeants would order the men to fall into line. The soldiers would count off each step of the required movements needed to complete the loading of their muskets. They took careful aim and squeezed the triggers. The best shooters received special rewards. A great deal of time was also spent learning how to use the lance, the sword, and even the bow and arrow. Many of the training exercises took place on horseback, because the soldiers would often fight battles while riding.

The soldiers had to learn many things that were not included in their drills. For example, they had to understand how to find water and shelter in the desert. Soldiers had to learn how to stay quiet and hidden when they were away from the presidios. They also had to memorize many rules about how they were supposed to act, including how to salute an officer.

Discipline

Everyone had to obey the rules. The drill sergeant hit anyone who did not follow orders with a short stick, called a *vara*. If a person broke a minor law, he or she would be placed in the stocks. These were large, wooden frames that held a person's arms, legs, and head tightly in place. A person would have to sit for hours as neighbors came by and made nasty comments. A jail

Reenactors, or living historians, try to show accurately what life was like at the missions and presidios. In this photograph, the soldiers at the right carry guns and lances. They are dressed in the common uniform of soldiers in California.

 23

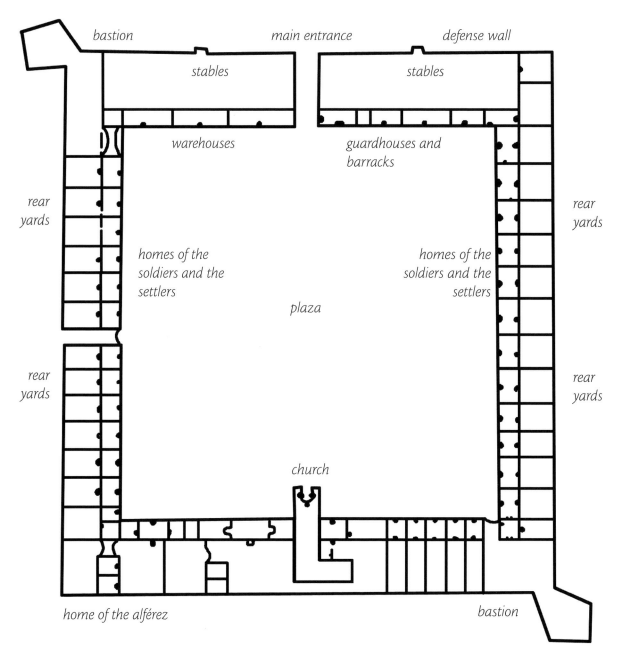

bastion   main entrance   defense wall

stables   stables

warehouses   guardhouses and barracks

rear yards

homes of the soldiers and the settlers

plaza

homes of the soldiers and the settlers

rear yards

rear yards

rear yards

church

home of the alférez   bastion

This is a plan of the Presidio of Santa Bárbara, as it appeared around 1788.

cell waited for anyone who broke a major law. The prisoners would have to help repair public buildings and clean the plaza. People who committed a more serious offense were whipped. For murder or running away from the army, one faced death by firing squad.

Presidio Duties

The soldiers had many military jobs. Some of this work took place at the presidios. The soldiers helped to build their presidios. The first temporary structures included a stockade and some crude, wooden houses. Buildings made from adobe bricks and tiles soon replaced these huts. The men worked hard to combine soil, water, and straw to make hundreds of thousands of bricks. The completed presidios included protecting walls called ramparts, a church, a commander's house, towerlike bastions, a guardhouse, warehouses, barracks, and homes for the married troops and settlers.

Every soldier had to stand guard duty. Each man arrived at the guardhouse with all of his military equipment. For the next 24 hours, a team of three guards would watch the prisoners in the jail and would walk around the ramparts, looking for enemies. The guards shouted, "*¿Quién está ahí?*," or "Who goes there?," to anyone who approached the gate. People traveling away from their homes had to carry a special letter from the government that explained what they were doing and where they were going. It was a soldier's job to arrest anyone who did not have the proper papers. While on duty, the men kept careful track of time. They rang a bell that sounded out the hours. At night they also took turns sleeping.

The officers regularly inspected the bases. They ordered the common soldiers to sweep and to clean the buildings. The officers also made sure that the troops took care of the weapons and the ammunition stored in the arsenals. The arms had to be cleaned and oiled at least once a month. The presidio's cannons also required special care. The army had to replace the wooden gun carriages on the cannons every few years. The soldiers had to roll the barrels of gunpowder across the room at least once a month to keep the powder from spoiling. Added to all of this, the presidio settlers were often ordered to make repairs to buildings damaged by the earthquakes and the violent storms common to the area.

The soldiers also worked as detectives and police. They had to be ready to investigate crimes and to arrest suspects. Officers served as judges and lawyers. Everyone from the surrounding areas went to the presidios to watch the trials. Commanders carefully recorded everything that happened during these events.

Duties Away from the Presidios

Many military duties took soldiers away from their bases. The areas outside the Spanish settlements were extremely dangerous. There was always a chance that a bandit, an enemy Indian, or a wild animal might become a threat.

The presidio troops also worked to keep the highways safe. Groups of soldiers escorted almost every traveler. The men also rode the highways during their regular patrols. They kept their eyes open for signs of crime or enemy

This is a page from the court records of a murder trial that took place at the Presidio of San Diego in 1808.

Year of 1808

Royal Presidio
of San Diego
criminal case
against the
mission Indians
named Francisco,
Fermin, and
Fernando of the
mission of San
Diego accused
of having murdered
the person Pedro
Miguel Alvarez on
the seventh of the
month of September

Judge and Ensign
Don Ignacio
Martinez

This watercolor by Ignacio Tirsch, painted around 1765, shows a man forcing a bull to lie down.

activity. Eventually each man also had to take a turn at delivering the mail. The troops carried all official letters and most of the personal letters written by the people who lived in the presidios and the pueblos.

Many of the troops also took a turn at working at the presidio ranches. The soldiers spent most of their time doing the jobs of cowboys, or vaqueros. They took care of the government-owned horses and cattle. The soldiers protected the creatures from wild animals, such as coyotes and bears. The men also had to round up and brand, or mark, the animals with hot irons. The ranch hands also trained the presidio horses. It took many months to produce an effective warhorse. This was important work. The presidios depended on their horses as much as they did on their men.

Some soldiers were stationed at the coastal forts, or *castillos*. The men trained for hours with the cannons. If they hit an enemy ship, the cannonballs would rip through its sails or decks. A lucky shot might even send the ship to the bottom. Aside from maintaining the cannons, which required endless care, there was not much to do except to wait for the next gun drill.

Every soldier lived in anticipation of going on a long campaign. It was exciting to play a part in an expedition that was arranged to fight Indians or to explore new regions. All soldiers had to take a lot of equipment with them. These items included extra food, water, ammunition, bedding, and tents. The troops also had to bring heavy cannons. Every man was supposed to report to the plaza with six horses and a mule. The troops were usually divided into three groups. The advance team served as scouts. Even the smallest fire might give away the army's position to the enemy, so smoking cigarettes and setting up campfires were not allowed. Sometimes the troops would muffle the sound of the horses' hoofs by wrapping them in leather or cloth. If the soldiers were lucky, they would catch their enemy asleep in their camps. When they went into battle, they shouted, *"¡Santiago y a ellos!,"* or, "Saint James and at them!" This was the same battle cry that had been used by the Spanish army since the Middle Ages. James, one of Jesus' 12 apostles, was seen as a religious savior by the Spaniards. He became a figure for them to rally around during war.

A Soldier's Life Off Duty

Many of the soldiers got time off from their army duties to work as civilians. California was a very isolated part of the Spanish Empire. Supplies of food and other necessary items took months, and sometimes years, to arrive. The colonists had to be as self-sufficient as possible. As time passed, large numbers of full-time civilian craftspeople, farmers, and ranchers also moved into the presidios. Civilian jobs could be found both inside the presidio walls and in the surrounding countryside.

Civilian Activities

Most of the married soldiers worked as part-time farmers and ranchers on their own land. Their chores took them away from the presidios, into the nearby fields and pastures. If a soldier could not get permission to take time off, his family had to do the work without him. If he had enough money, the soldier could hire Indians or other settlers to help.

The chores that had to be done at the private ranches were similar to those that had to be done at the government ranches. The colonists' livestock provided milk, cheese, and meat, as well as other useful items, such as leather and wool. Most of the larger animals were allowed to graze in the vast stretches of wild grasslands that surrounded the presidios. The types of livestock that

William Smyth made sketches of various California scenes while on an expedition led by Captain Frederick William Beechey to the Pacific Ocean and the Bering Strait in the mid 1820s. This illustration, "Californians Throwing the Lasso," is based on one of Smyth's sketches.

were kept included cattle, horses, mules, sheep, and goats. Raising livestock required many hours of hard labor. The hills around the presidios were filled with grizzly bears, wild bulls, other dangerous beasts, and sometimes enemy Indians. Cattle and horses often stampeded when they heard an unexpected sound, such as thunder. More than one soldier died while looking after the herds.

These are water channels at Mission San Luis Rey in California.

The three most important crops on the presidio farms were wheat, corn, and barley. The colonists also had fields of many other kinds of vegetables. Of equal importance were the settlers' orchards of fruit trees and olives. An elaborate system of canals, or *acequias*, provided water to the plants. During the planting and the harvest, the colonists worked from sunrise to sunset. Some families built temporary homes in their fields, or they slept in the open, under the stars.

Many colonists spent their spare time hunting and fishing. Others collected extra food by gathering shellfish and wild, edible plants. The plentiful wild foods meant that anyone who was willing to do the work of collecting food could find enough to eat.

The married soldiers also found jobs within the presidio walls. Many worked as professional craftsmen. Those who could read and could write often became secretaries for the officers, or made extra money writing letters for other settlers.

Presidio Homes

The unmarried soldiers lived together in long, narrow buildings called barracks. Long, wide benches lined the walls. These platforms served as beds. Each man had his own mat, blankets, and pillows. The men cooked their food outside using stone or adobe stoves and ovens. A sergeant, who had his own room, was put in charge of the barracks.

The married soldiers lived with their families in small, privately owned homes. Few houses included more than two rooms and a small attic. Furniture consisted of little more than a crude table, a few chairs, and mats that served as beds. As many as a dozen people might live together in these small rooms.

The houses of the officers and the wealthier families were larger and more comfortable than were those of the common soldiers. Some of the commanders' houses had as many as eight rooms with fancy wooden beds, chairs, sofas, and tables. Paintings and mirrors often decorated the walls.

Home Entertainment

A great deal of time was spent in the company of family and friends. The presidio communities enjoyed many different kinds of entertainment. Games of all types were extremely popular. People living in the presidios often played card games, dice games, checkers, backgammon, and chess. Many of the colonists gambled on the outcomes of these contests.

Informal dance parties provided one of the most important forms of entertainment. Everyone joined in the celebrations. The parties included singing, and playing a guitar or a violin. There were many popular songs about love and adventure. The dances came from all over the world, including Spain, Mexico, the Philippines, and Africa. The parties helped to

California settlers brought many dance traditions from Spain and Mexico. In this illustration, a woman dances to the music of a guitar.

make everyone feel as though they belonged to a larger, extended family of California settlers.

The wealthy settlers enjoyed more refined forms of entertainment. Song recitals accompanied by guitars provided opportunities for the officers and their wives to hear the latest European favorites. There were fancy balls where the participants wore costumes and masks. New arrivals brought news about what was going on in Mexico and in Spain. The ships that brought supplies also delivered books and magazines from Europe. The adults would take turns reading them aloud to their families and dinner guests.

A Soldier's Life at the Missions

There were almost as many soldiers working at the missions as there were working at the presidios. In many ways, the mission settlements were very different from the military bases, and daily life for the soldiers working there was different, too. The missions were run by the Franciscan priests. The settlements usually had more buildings than did the presidios. Most settlements also had thousands of Indians who had their own way of life. The men that served in the missions were much more isolated than were those that lived in the presidios and the pueblos. Usually the only people at a mission who were not local Indians were the priests, a few hired craftsmen, the soldiers, and the soldiers' families. For example, at Mission San Luis Rey in southern California, there were about 30 colonists and more than 2,500 Indians.

Assignment to a mission could last for a few weeks or for many years. If they were going to have to stay for a long time, the soldiers moved their families to live with them at the mission. The houses in which the soldiers stayed at the mission were similar to those found in the presidios.

The work that the mission soldiers did was different from the assignments given to the army at the presidio. A mission soldier's main job was to protect the priests and the Indians. Serious threats to the mission's security were rare, so the soldiers spent most of their time helping the Franciscans and working as

A soldier talks with Indians in front of the soldiers' barracks at the Carmel presidio in this 1827 Richard Beechey painting.

teachers. They taught the Indians many new skills, including how to be cowboys and farmers. The Franciscan missionaries often hired the soldiers' wives to teach methods of European housekeeping and cooking.

Soldiers also had the important job of organizing and training the mission Indians as a kind of militia. The Indians needed to be prepared to fight if California was ever invaded. This was very important, because there were so few regular soldiers available. Without this militia, a European enemy, or even a large group of enemy Indians, easily could have captured California.

Sometimes the soldiers would act as policemen and would help local Indian officials enforce the mission rules. People who broke the rules were usually put into the stocks, but the guardhouse also included a small jail. The soldiers also arrested murderers and other serious criminals, who then had to stand trial at the presidios. Soldiers who hurt the Indians were arrested and punished.

The Franciscans sometimes hired soldiers to do extra work as supervisors. These men would lead the Indians in construction, ranching, and farming. Many of the foremen made a lot of money doing their work as supervisors.

Many of the soldiers liked the Franciscans and the Indians. Some men married native girls. The soldiers' children played together and learned Indian languages as well as native ways of doing things. Other soldiers used their time at the missions to make money. Not everyone was happy, though. Some soldiers hated having to go to church every day. They said that the priests had too many rules. At the presidios, the Franciscan priests rarely visited more than once a week. The unhappy soldiers at the missions missed their independence.

The Women of the Military Families

The presidios included more women colonists than soldiers. Women had many different jobs. They served as homemakers, craftspeople, and tradespeople. They worked at a variety of trades alongside their husbands. Their efforts were essential to the presidios' survival.

Work in the House

The lives of most women were focused on the home. Each day there were many chores. All the women and the children helped out. Cooking consisted of a time-consuming, backbreaking set of jobs. Women spent hours bent over slabs of stone, called metates, rocking heavy grinders, called manos, back and forth to grind wheat and corn into flour. The women also sweated in their hot kitchens as they cooked food in pots, pans, and flat trays, called *comales*. Every home had its own stove, and often several houses shared a large oven. The pottery used to serve food came from faraway places, including central Mexico, China, and Europe.

The women were responsible for preparing and preserving the food. Fruits and vegetables were dried for use in the winter. Animals killed for food had to be cleaned and cut into pieces. The men removed the hide, or fur and skin. The women then cut the meat from the animal's body. Though some of

the meat was cooked right away, most of it was dried for later use. The settlers cut the flesh into long strips. The pieces were dipped in salt and then were hung from poles and ropes and stored in a warehouse. The settlers also boiled the animal's body fat to make tallow. Tallow was used for many things, including candles and grease for the axles of carts. Almost no part of the animal was wasted.

Many hours were spent cleaning the home. The women used reed and grass brooms to sweep the floors. They also scrubbed the dishes and filled the oil lamps. The oldest woman took care of the family shrine, decorating it with flowers and candles. Women were also responsible for keeping the family clothes and linen clean. They hauled the laundry to the closest source of running water. The cloth objects were beaten and scrubbed with soap and water to remove the dirt before being rinsed. Then women hung the wet fabrics on trees or clotheslines to dry.

Women made thread with a spinning wheel, such as this replica at Mission La Purísima.

The women also created many household products, including clothing. They were famous for their fine embroidery and delicate fringe work. Garments wore out rapidly, so the women also made repairs with needles and thread.

◄ *A woman grinds grains on a stone to make bread.*

In addition to all of their other chores, women were responsible for taking care of the household's smaller animals. Some of these creatures, such as parrots, cats, and dogs, were pets. Other small animals, such as chickens, doves, turkeys, and pigs, were kept for food or were sold to increase the family's income.

Most married women were responsible for the family budget. They decided when and how the money would be spent. Because they had to keep track of purchases, they often learned to read, to write, and to do simple arithmetic.

Work Outside the House

According to Spanish traditions, proper women did not work outside the home. However, the lack of settlers in California created opportunities for women that otherwise would have been impossible. Presidio wives and daughters could be found in the fields working alongside their husbands and male children. Some women ran their family ranches and farms. In some cases, this was because their husbands and sons were away. However, some women chose not to marry and made a living doing these occupations. All females helped to hunt and to collect shellfish and useful wild plants. Many of the older single women worked as gardeners, bakers, weavers, laundry workers, and tailors. Some of the ladies even worked in medicine. Many became recognized *curanderas*, or folk doctors, and others became midwives, or people who help women to give birth.

Growing Up in a Military Family

The presidios were not just homes to men and women. Hundreds of children also lived there. Their lives were very different from their parents' lives.

The presidio families, like families today, came in many different sizes. A person could have as many as one dozen brothers and sisters. However, most families had three or fewer children. It was a difficult life. Because of death and shifting job assignments, there were many single-parent families. Sometimes grandparents, aunts, and uncles shared a family's home.

The youngest infants spent their days with their mothers. Older brothers or sisters often supervised the toddlers. The older children spent their spare time with neighborhood friends.

When a child turned four, he or she was given chores to do. The smaller children watched the family animals, helped to take care of their younger brothers and sisters, protected crops by driving birds from the fields, and brought water to their houses. As a child grew up, parents expected him or her to help out with the same jobs that adults did. By the time children turned 15, they knew how to do most of the tasks of daily life. However, they were not considered to be adults until they were married. Most girls married between the ages of 15 and 21. The boys were usually a few years older than the girls were when they got married.

Education

The children of early California had to learn about many things that we do not have to understand today. Parents and older family members provided most of a youngster's education. Learning to live on the frontier was hard work and took many years to master. Both boys and girls learned by doing.

Everyone had to know how to ride a horse. As soon as a baby could leave the house, he or she began to learn to sit in a saddle. Presidio children grew up surrounded by adults who spoke many different languages. Most of the youngsters learned to speak Spanish, several Indian languages, and sometimes Basque and Catalan, dialects from different regions of Spain.

The lack of people in California made it necessary for everyone to learn how to do everything. If a person could not do a job for himself, there was often no one else to do it for him. Boys learned how to cook and to sew. Girls learned how to ride, to shoot guns, and to pack saddles.

During the evenings, the older children listened to folktales. These stories provided many lessons about what was right and wrong. At least once a month, the children would go to a class on religion taught by priests who came from the nearby missions. The children's parents also spent many hours explaining the importance of their faith.

Good manners were also taught, as were special rules of behavior. Children were not allowed to speak to adults unless they were spoken to. They could not sit down if an adult was standing. Boys were taught to take off their hats before they spoke. A child was taught never to stare into an

◄ *Presidio women acted as teachers for the young girls. Here girls are shown going with their teacher to the top of a hill to gather the precious fruit called pitahaya.*  45

adult's eyes. When children spoke to their parents, they had to use special, polite words and phrases. If a young person ignored the rules, he or she was punished just as children sometimes are today.

The Presidio Schools

One had to be able to read and write to become an officer, or to understand a land deed. A woman needed to understand arithmetic to take care of her family's money. To prepare children for these duties, the adults understood that their offspring needed a formal education. If the parents could not teach them, families sometimes hired special tutors.

Eventually the Spanish king ordered the creation of schools at the presidios. By 1800, each of the presidios had a classroom. The students rarely numbered more than 30. The classes combined several grades. At first only boys were allowed to attend, but girls got their own school at the Monterey presidio before 1820. The bell starting the school day rang at 8:00 A.M. At 11:00 A.M., everyone went home for lunch. Classes started again after the siesta at 3:00 P.M. By 5:00 P.M. the school day ended. The students had to attend classes six days a week, Monday through Saturday. The last day of the week was set aside for taking tests. The school year was broken up by many holidays. In all, students spent less time in the classroom than students spend today.

The schoolhouse was a large adobe building. At one end of the room there was a desk and a chair for the teacher. The students sat on wooden benches. They usually didn't have desks. Most of the light entered the room from the door or from a few small windows found in the upper walls. It was very cold in the schoolhouse during the winter, and it could be terribly hot in the summer.

The lessons covered reading, writing, arithmetic, religion, and history. They composed their first exercises using slate boards and chalk. In time students graduated to the use of feather pens and ink. It was hard work to control the pen. Students learned to pour sand on their assignments to make sure that the writing would not smudge. They memorized sayings and recited them in class when the teachers called on them. Some of the instructors rewarded students who did well with candy, dried fruit, and nuts. If a child forgot an assignment or broke the rules, he or she was punished with a slap or was hit with a whip or a stick.

This kind of printed table was used to teach spelling.

All the students' papers were collected at the end of the day. The paper was wrapped around lead balls and then tied or twisted closed, to make cartridges for the soldiers' pistols and muskets. Nothing was wasted. At the end of the school year, the teachers gave grades to the students. The students who did not learn their lessons had to repeat the previous year's instruction.

Entertainment

Although adults and children had a lot of work to do, time was set aside for play. The colonists made most of their children's toys. At a typical presidio, children played with wooden hobbyhorses, dolls, or *muñecas*, and peashooters. Many different games were popular. The children shouted as their wooden tops and clay marbles crashed together. Other games included jacks, hopscotch, and blindman's buff. Many contests involved riddles, clapping, and songs. In one game, a person rolled a wooden hoop for as long as possible using a stick. When they could get them, children also played with cards and dice. More often than not, though, they used locally made versions created out of flowers, scraps of paper, and wood. Buttons replaced coins in gambling games. Everyone learned to sing and to dance. Many evenings were spent listening to folktales and riddles. The night was often filled with the sounds of children singing traditional Spanish, Mexican, and Indian songs, accompanied by drums and guitars.

Religion and the Military Families

All the people who lived at the presidio were members of the same church. Everyone was Roman Catholic. Christianity was very important to the colonists. There were prayers and ceremonies for almost everything that they did. Even the people who did not believe in God had to go to church. Otherwise they were fined and might even be put in jail.

Most of the people loved their church. It held so many interesting and beautiful ceremonies. Holidays provided endless fun, and the weekly church service was an opportunity for everyone to get together. It comforted people to think that God, the saints, and the angels were looking after them.

The church building was the biggest, nicest structure in the presidio. These churches looked different from modern churches. Inside there were no benches. During religious services, everyone either stood up or kneeled. All the men and the boys stood on one side of the church. Girls and women stood on the other side. During the day, light poured through small windows in the walls. At night hundreds of candles cast mysterious shadows. Paintings and statues of saints covered the walls and the altars. This place made most people feel proud and special.

This is a crucifix from the San Diego presidio.

None of the presidios had their own priest, but a Franciscan missionary came to the settlements each Sunday to say Mass. The ceremonies helped the colonists to live good lives and to understand their religion better. There were many special prayers and beautiful songs. Everything that took place inside the church was different from the rest of the colonists' life. The

Religious statues, such as this statue of the Madonna and Child from the Santa Bárbara Mission church, were meant to remind the colonists of people and lessons in the Bible and in Roman Catholic teachings.

ceremonies helped people to feel connected to other frontier families in a meaningful way and allowed them to express their belief in God in a spiritual setting.

The church was designed to make the settlers feel closer to God.
◄ *The church altar at Santa Bárbara is an example of the ornate designs and religious sculptures found in many mission and presidio churches.*

Not all the religious ceremonies took place at church. Most settlers created some kind of shrine in their homes. Here they kept their religious pictures or statues of saints. The day began and ended with the lighting of candles and the reading of prayers. Most settlers also wore crosses or carried other religious objects to help them remember the teachings of their religion. Because the priests were rarely present, the families organized many ceremonies and provided a great deal of the children's religious educations themselves.

The Religious Fiestas

The most exciting days of the year were usually the religious holidays. All work would stop, and there would be special ceremonies followed by parties that could go on for several days. Work was hard on the frontier, but they actually had more days off than we have today.

Many of the holidays involved sacred parades, private sacrifices, and prayers for forgiveness. However, by no means were all the ceremonies serious. Some of the holidays were wild celebrations. The colonists made fun of the devil and his demons through songs, dances, and plays. The celebrations were a source of community pride. The colonists worked for weeks to prepare for major holidays. The women collected flowers with which to decorate the church and the family shrine. Men cut branches to beautify the outsides of the presidio buildings. The families gathered together the ingredients of special holiday foods.

On the most important holidays, there usually would be some kind of special show and dance. The celebrations often began with a parade. In the plaza, the colonists held bullfights, horse races, and contests between wild bulls and grizzly bears. Sometimes there would be special dramatic performances that enacted stories from the Bible. Celebrations went on into the early hours of the morning in the light created by dozens of roaring bonfires. By the end of the mission era, around 1835, groups of performers known as *maromeros* added to the celebrations. They performed short, funny plays and gave demonstrations of juggling and acrobatics.

Leaving the Army

When a man joined the army, he had to promise to stay in it for at least eight years. At the end of that time, he could either sign up for another term or retire. If a soldier decided to leave the army, he sold his weapons and other equipment to the government. Retired soldiers did not have to leave the presidios. As long as they lived at the base, they had the right to the homes and the lands that they had been granted. Soldiers and their families could still receive care from army doctors, and the men were automatically made a part of the militia. After from 18 to 25 years in the army, a soldier also received a special monthly bonus payment. Most of the retired military men continued to live in California and made a living as cattle ranchers.

Not everyone was able to complete their term of service. Sometimes a man would become seriously sick. In battle, men often suffered horrible wounds. Whatever the cause, if a person was too sick to serve, he was allowed to retire with pay and to continue to receive army medical care.

Sometimes an unhappy soldier would run away. These men were called deserters. The skills that they had learned in the army made them dangerous thieves. If caught the deserters had to stand trial. Sometimes they were shot, hanged, or beaten to death. If a man had a good excuse for running away, he might just be thrown in jail and then forced to leave the army without benefits.

Many retired soldiers wanted to become wealthy ranchers, like the man shown in the foreground here. ➤

If a soldier died while in service, he was given special honors by the government. His family was given all his retirement benefits, including pay and land grants. His weapons and other military gear were purchased by the commanding officer to be sold to the new men who joined.

The Presidio Heritage

What would have happened if there had never been a California presidio system? No one can answer this question. It is clear that the presidios' story continues to echo across the centuries in California's laws, its geography, and even in the faces of its people. The descendants of families that came to early California and that lived on the presidios still can be found in every major city in the state. Spanish is still spoken in the cities and the towns that were born as presidios.

In a very real way, the vanished presidios have lived on. They represent a heritage that the United States shares with Spain and Mexico.

This is Spain's royal coat of arms.

San Francisco Solano

San Rafael Arcángel

San José

Presidio
de San
Francisco

Santa Clara de Asís

Pueblo de San José

Santa Cruz

San Juan Bautista

Presidio de
San Carlos

San Carlos Borromeo
de Carmelo

Nuestra Señora de la Soledad

San Antonio de Padua

San Miguel Arcángel

San Luis Obispo de Tolosa

La Purísima Concepción

Santa Inés

Santa Bárbara

Presidio de Santa Bárbara

San Buenaventura

San Fernando
Rey de España

Pueblo de
Los Angeles

San Gabriel
Arcángel

San Juan
Capistrano

San Luis Rey
de Francia

Presidio de San Diego

San Diego
de Alcalá

Glossary

acequias (uh-SAY-kee-uhz) Aqueducts or irrigation ditches.

adobe (uh-DOH-bee) Brick made from dried mud and straw.

alférez (al-FER-es) The second in command of a presidio, who carried the presidio's flag into battle.

arsenals (AR-sih-nuhlz) Places where weapons and ammunition are stored.

artifacts (AR-tih-fakts) Objects that show evidence of human activity.

barracks (BAR-iks) Buildings used to house soldiers.

bastions (BAS-chuhnz) Strong points, usually constructed at a fort's corners. Some bastions were tall, like towers, although many were low and shaped like triangles.

brand (BRAND) A kind of iron pole with a design that was used to mark animals, such as cattle.

castillos (kas-TEE-yohs) In California, a term used for coastal forts that mounted large cannon.

cavalry (KA-vul-ree) Soldiers who fought on horseback.

comales (koh-MAL-ays) A tray made from metal or ceramics used to cook tortillas.

commission (kuh-MIH-shun) A special license to become an officer.

descendants (dih-SEN-dents) People who can trace their ancestors back to a particular person.

deserters (dih-ZERT-ers) Men who run away while serving with an army.

drilled (DRILD) Having done a set of repetitive exercises.

historical archaeology (hih-STOR-ih-kul ar-kee-AH-luh-jee) The study of the traces left behind by people living during the era of European expansion, from 1492 to the present.

manos (MAH-nohs) Grinding tools made from stone that are used to make cornmeal and similar powders.

maromeros (mar-oh-MER-ohs) Troops of performers that arrived in California at the end of the mission era, about 1824.

metates (meh-TAH-tayz) Curved stones against which one grinds grains with manos.

midwives (MID-wyvz) Special nurses who help when babies are born.

militia (muh-LIH-shuh) Part-time soldiers called up during a time of crisis.

muñecas (moo-NYAY-kuz) Dolls.

Norteños (nor-TAYN-yohs) Northerners. This was a term used for the people who lived on the northern frontier of New Spain, including Alta California.

presidios (preh-SEE-dee-ohz) Military colonies in northern New Spain. In California, all the presidios were protected by fortifications.

pueblos (PWAY-blohs) The Spanish word for villages.

ramparts (RAM-parts) Kinds of fortified walls with walkways that usually surrounded forts.

ranchos (RAHN-chohs) Stock raising settlements or farms.

ranks (RANKS) The different levels of authority for soldiers in the army. For example, a general is high ranking.

shrine (SHRYN) A special place at which prayers or memorials can be made.

siesta (see-ES-tuh) An afternoon break that usually lasted several hours.

soldados de cuera (sohl-DAH-dohs DAY KWEH-rah) Leather jacket soldiers.

stockade (stah-KAYD) A line of stout posts set firmly to form a defense, operating like a large fence.

stocks (STAHKS) A kind of wooden frame where a person has their legs, arms, or hands held in a tight grip.

tallow (TA-loh) A fatty substance used in candle making and as a kind of grease for lubrication.

vaqueros (vah-KER-ohs) Cowboys.

vara (VAR-uh) A stick used to beat men when they failed to perform an order. The term vara was also used for a measurement 2.73 feet (.8 m) in length.

Additional Resources

There are many places that you can learn more about early California and life in the presidios. The following lists provide information about some of the more important resources.

Books

Nelson, Libby and Kari Cornell. *Projects and Layouts: California Missions*. New York: Lerner Publications Company, 1997.

Van Steenwyk, Elizabeth. *The California Missions*. New York: Franklin Watts, 1998.

Museums

Santa Bárbara Presidio State Historic Park–Santa Bárbara Trust for Historic Preservation. 123 East Canon Perdido Street, Santa Bárbara, California 93101

This is the finest museum in the country that is dedicated to our understanding of the California presidios and their settlers.

Web Sites

Due to the changing nature of Internet links, PowerKids Press has developed an online list of Web sites related to the subject of this book. This site is updated regularly. Please use this link to access the list:

www.powerkidslinks.com/pcm/soldie/

Index

A

acequias, 32

Alta California, 5

anthropologists, 11

archaeologists, 11, 13

army,

joining, 17–18

leaving, 54

B

Baja California, 17

Britain, 10

C

Califia, 5

Carlos III, king of Spain, 6–7

children, 43

chores, 43

education, 45–47

entertainment, 48

marriage, 43

religious education, 52

Cortés, Hernán, 5

F

Franciscan(s), 7, 14, 37–38

G

Gálvez, José de, 6–8

J

Jefferson, Thomas, 10

L

leather jacket soldiers, 18

M

Mexico, 5, 7–8, 10, 34–35

mission(s), 7, 10–11, 20

daily life at, 37–38

missionaries, 7, 14

Mission San Luis Rey, 37

N

Norteños, 17

P

Philippines, the, 5, 17, 34

presidio(s), 7–8, 10–11, 14, 17–20, 25,
    32–33
    daily life at, 21, 23
    entertainment in, 33–35, 48
    homes in, 33
    Monterey, 14
    religion at, 49, 51–53
    San Diego, 14
    San Francisco, 14
    Santa Bárbara, 14
    schools at, 46–47

S

Serra, Junípero, 7, 9

Spain, 17, 34–35

Spanish Empire, 14, 20

stocks, 23, 38

T

tools, 11

W

Washington, George, 9–10

weapons, 11, 18–19, 23

women
    at presidios, 39
    budgeting, 42
    cleaning, 41
    cooking, 39, 41
    curanderas, 42
    fieldwork, 42
    reading, 42
    sewing, 41
    unmarried, 42
    writing, 42

About the Authors

Dr. Jack Stephen Williams has worked as an archaeologist and a historian on various research projects in the United States, Mexico, South America, and Europe. Williams has a particular interest in Native Americans and early colonization of the Southwest and California. He holds a doctoral degree in anthropology from the University of Arizona and has written numerous books and articles. Williams lives in San Diego with his wife, Anita G. Cohen-Williams, and his daughter, Louise.

Thomas L. Davis, M.Div, M.A., was first introduced to the California Missions in 1957, by his grandmother. He began to collect books, photos and any other materials about the missions. Over the years, he has assembled a first-class research library about the missions and Spanish North America and is a respected authority in his field. After 10 years working in the music business, Davis studied for the Catholic priesthood and was ordained for service in Los Angeles, California. ten years as a Roman Catholic priest saw Father Thom make another life change. He studied at U.C.L.A. and California State University, Northridge, where he received his M.A. in history. He is a founding member of the California Mission Studies Association and teaches California and Latin America History at the College of the Canyons, Santa Clarita, California. Davis lives in Palmdale, California, with his wife, Rebecca, and son, Graham.